C000094128

THE GREAT LITTLE BOOK OF OUTDOOR RECIPES

it's a **picnic**

THE GREAT LITTLE BOOK OF OUTDOOR RECIPES

it's a **picnic**

emma summer

southwater

This edition is published by Southwater

Southwater is an imprint of Anness Publishing Ltd
Hermes House, 88–89 Blackfriars Road, London SE1 8HA
tel. 020 7401 2077; fax 020 7633 9499
www.southwaterbooks.com; info@anness.com

© Anness Publishing Ltd 1998, 2004

UK agent: The Manning Partnership Ltd, 6 The Old Dairy, Melcombe Road, Bath BA2 3LR;
tel. 01225 478444; fax 01225 478440; sales@manning-partnership.co.uk

UK distributor: Grantham Book Services Ltd, Isaac Newton Way, Alma Park Industrial Estate, Grantham, Lincs NG31 9SD;
tel. 01476 541080; fax 01476 541061; orders@gbs.tbs-ltd.co.uk

North American agent/distributor: National Book Network, 4501 Forbes Boulevard, Suite 200, Lanham, MD 20706;
tel. 301 459 3366; fax 301 429 5746; www.nbnbooks.com

Australian agent/distributor: Pan Macmillan Australia, Level 18, St Martins Tower, 31 Market St, Sydney, NSW 2000;
tel. 1300 135 113; fax 1300 135 103; customer.service@macmillan.com.au

New Zealand agent/distributor: David Bateman Ltd, 30 Tarndale Grove, Off Bush Road, Albany, Auckland;
tel. (09) 415 7664; fax (09) 415 8892

All rights reserved. No part of this publication may be reproduced, stored in a retrieval system,
or transmitted in any way or by any means, electronic, mechanical, photocopying,
recording or otherwise, without the prior written permission of the copyright holder.

A CIP catalogue record for this book is available from the British Library.

Publisher Joanna Lorenz
Editor Sarah Ainley
Copy Editor Jenni Fleetwood
Designers Patrick McLeavey & Jo Brewer
Illustrator Anna Koska
Photographers Edward Allwright, James Duncan, Michelle Garrett,
Amanda Heywood, Tim Hill & Debbie Patterson
Recipes Carla Capalbo, Jacqueline Clark, Carole Clements, Matthew Drennan,
Joanna Farrow, Carole Handslip, Sarah Maxwell, Angela Nilson,
Liz Trigg, Steven Wheeler & Elizabeth Wolf-Cohen

Previously published as *The Perfect Picnic Cookbook*

1 3 5 7 9 10 8 6 4 2

NOTES

For all recipes, quantities are given in both metric and imperial measures and, where appropriate,
measures are also given in standard cups and spoons. Follow one set, but not a mixture, because they are not interchangeable.

Standard spoon and cup measures are level.

1 tsp = 5ml, 1 tbsp = 15ml, 1 cup = 250ml/8fl oz

Australian standard tablespoons are 20ml. Australian readers should use
3 tsp in place of 1 tbsp for measuring small quantities of gelatine, flour, salt, etc.

Medium (US large) eggs are used unless otherwise stated.

Contents

Introduction

Pack up a picnic and pursue one of life's most delightful pleasures. Despite – or because of – the vagaries of the weather and the other uncertainties associated with eating out, such as whether the midges will be massing or the ants preparing for an all-out assault, eating out of doors never fails to be an adventure. Whether you stick a few sandwiches and a couple of apples in a backpack, or spread out a banquet by a babbling brook, there's always something special about eating in the open air.

The Victorians loved a lavish picnic and thought nothing of toting to the site huge, groaning hampers containing everything from whole joints of roast meat, dressed crab and lobster, salads and savouries to elaborate puddings and cakes.

The traditional Victorian picnic feast would include the obligatory cucumber sandwiches followed by cricket and croquet, with games for the children and adults dozing in the warm afternoon sunshine.

The advent of the barbecue pushed picnics into second place for a while, but in recent years there has been a revival and today picnics are being appreciated more and more as a wonderful way of combining social entertaining with enjoyment of the countryside. Kitchenware companies have been quick to appreciate this, and there is now a vast range of equipment available to the dedicated picnicker. There seems to be a suitable container for every type and shape of food, some with separate compartments for sauces and dressings, and chiller boxes and bags to carry them in. Unbreakable steel flasks are invaluable for hot and cold drinks; choose a wide-mouthed flask for soups to make pouring that much easier.

While such equipment is by no means essential, it can make a huge difference to the success of your picnic. If you foresee no handy stream to cool your champagne in, pack it in a special insulated bag, and when pouring the champagne, avoid spills by using spiked wine glasses that stick firmly in the ground. Picnic tableware should be bright and colourful to compete with the glories of nature. Have place settings in individual colours for each guest, to make plates and knives more easily identifiable.

A good idea is to pack plenty of cushions and back-rests – there's nothing worse than trying to eat a meal when you are horribly uncomfortable – and pack a couple of garden chairs for older guests. Picnic rugs are pretty, but often too small for a large crowd. An old bedsheet may be more practical, and will certainly be easier to wash. Spread a few bin bags underneath it to keep the worst of the damp and dirt at bay, then use the bags for taking away your rubbish when the picnic is over.

Better insulated containers may have improved food safety, but there's no room for complacency. There's little point in carefully keeping food chilled if you later leave it standing in the sunshine for several hours. Pack any uneaten food away quickly: you can always get it out again.

Always take care to leave the picnic site as pristine as possible. Make fires only in designated areas, and if you light candles for illumination or to keep insects away, make sure they can't be knocked over.

Most of all, you should sit back, relax and enjoy the delicious food and the company. That's the real enjoyment of eating out!

Perfect Picnic Fare

BREADS

The original convenience food. Bake your own – it's so simple with easy-blend dried yeast – or raid the bakery. Baps and bagels become sophisticated snacks with interesting fillings, and pitta pockets are perfect for holding falafel or salads.

CAKES AND BAKES

It is best to avoid gooey icings but fruit cakes and loaves are ideal. Pack them in the tin in which they were baked.

CRUDITÉS

Pack a selection of crisp raw vegetables, cut into slim sticks or strips or broken into florets. Include carrots, radishes, cauliflower, peppers of every colour, spring onions, firm baby button mushrooms and cucumber. Serve with hummus, taramasalata or tzatziki.

DESSERTS

Light, fresh and pretty – that's the only recipe for the perfect picnic dessert. Avoid anything too fragile, and keep cream-based puddings well chilled.

DRESSINGS

Pack oil-based dressings in leakproof beakers and shake just before adding to salads. Use bought mayonnaise for picnics, rather than making your own.

DRINKS

It is easy to underestimate how much people drink in the open air. Take plenty of fruit juices and bottled water as well as wine and beer for non-drivers, if wanted. Use unbreakable flasks for hot drinks like coffee, tea or hot chocolate.

FRUIT

Fresh berry fruits, packed in baskets (with leaves), look lovely for a summer picnic.

8

PASTRIES

Individual pastries, like tartlets, pasties and filo kerchiefs, are easy to eat, and you can include several different fillings. A large pie makes an impressive centrepiece.

PÂTÉS

A rough country pâté is a good addition to the feast, but must be kept chilled. Avoid chicken liver pâté, which is too perishable.

PIZZAS

For a quick and easy treat, make up a batch of pizza dough and cut out small rounds with biscuit cutters. Spread with home-made tomato sauce, add the topping of your choice, then sprinkle with a mixture of grated Cheddar and mozzarella. Bake at 220°C/425°F/Gas 7 for 15 minutes.

SALADS

Made for outdoor eating, salads can be simple or elaborate. Garnishes, croûtons and sprinkles (like toasted nuts or seeds) are easy to pack and turn a simple salad into something special.

SOUPS

Cold soups, such as gazpacho or vichyssoise, are ideal for a hot day, whereas winter looks a shade warmer when viewed over a steaming cup of minestrone. Transport soups in wide-mouthed flasks and include bowls and spoons.

CHECKLIST

- Corkscrew
- Napkins
- Salt and pepper
- Kitchen paper
- Damp flannels or wipes
- Chopping board
- Serving spoons and lifters
- Knives for food preparation
- Sunscreen
- Insect repellent
- Bin bags

9

Techniques

PREPARING SALAD LEAVES

Wash and drain the leaves. Break off any tough ribs. Dry robust leaves in a salad spinner; blot delicate leaves with kitchen paper. Pack the leaves into polythene bags, close tightly and store in the fridge before packing in a chiller bag.

MIXING BLUE CHEESE DRESSING

Remove the rind from 75g/3oz Stilton and crumble the cheese into a bowl. Beat in 150ml/$\frac{1}{4}$ pint/$\frac{2}{3}$ cup natural yogurt, with 45ml/3 tbsp olive oil and 30ml/2 tbsp lemon juice. Sprinkle with fresh chives. Season well.

MAKING FRENCH DRESSING

Mix 90ml/6 tbsp extra-virgin olive oil and 15ml/1 tbsp white wine vinegar in a screw-top jar. Add 5ml/1 tsp French mustard and a pinch of caster sugar. Close the jar tightly and shake well. Shake again before dressing the salad.

MAKING GARLIC CROÛTONS

Cut the crusts off 3 slices of day-old bread; slice the bread into small cubes. Heat 60ml/4 tbsp olive oil in a frying pan and fry the shapes until crisp and golden. Sprinkle with salt and drain on kitchen paper. Pack in an airtight tub.

Simple Sandwich Fillings

AVOCADO & SPRING ONION

Cut an avocado in half and remove the stone and peel. Mash the flesh until smooth, then beat in 1 chopped spring onion and 10ml/ 2 tsp lemon juice. Season with a dash of Worcestershire sauce and then add plenty of salt and pepper.

TUNA & TOMATO

Drain a 75g/3oz can of tuna. Flake the fish with a fork. Add 25g/1oz/2 tbsp softened butter, 15ml/1 tbsp tomato ketchup and 15ml/1 tbsp mayonnaise. Mix well, then add salt and pepper to taste.

EGG & CRESS

Shell 2 hard-boiled eggs and chop them finely. Add 50g/2oz/¼ cup full-fat soft cheese and 30ml/2 tbsp mayonnaise. Mix well, then snip in the tops from a carton of mustard and cress. Season well with salt and pepper.

ONION WITH SPINACH & CHEESE

Chop an onion and fry in olive oil until golden. Allow to cool. Layer the onion on granary baps with raw spinach leaves and grated Cheddar cheese mixed with a little mayonnaise.

SMOKED SALMON & GRAVLAX SAUCE

Mix 25g/1oz/2 tbsp butter with 5ml/1 tsp grated lemon zest and spread over 4 slices of rye bread. Cover with 100g/4oz smoked salmon and add a curly endive leaf and a lemon slice. Spoon over 60ml/4 tbsp Gravlax Sauce. Garnish each portion with a sprig of fresh dill.

FRANKFURTER & POTATO SALAD

Mix 115g/4oz/⅔ cup potato salad with 2 finely chopped spring onions. Use as a sandwich filling with 2 sliced frankfurters and 2 sliced tomatoes.

PARMA HAM, PESTO & MOZZARELLA

Stir 30ml/2 tbsp pesto into 60ml/4 tbsp mayonnaise. Use as a filling for bridge rolls, adding sliced Parma ham, mozzarella and vine tomatoes. Add some shredded fresh basil, if you like.

Finger Food

Falafel

INGREDIENTS

150g / 5oz / ¾ cup dried chick-peas
1 large onion, roughly chopped
2 garlic cloves, roughly chopped
60ml / 4 tbsp roughly chopped fresh parsley
5ml / 1 tsp ground cumin
5ml / 1 tsp ground coriander
2.5ml / ½ tsp baking powder
oil for deep-frying
salt and ground black pepper
pitta bread, salad and yogurt, to serve

SERVES 4

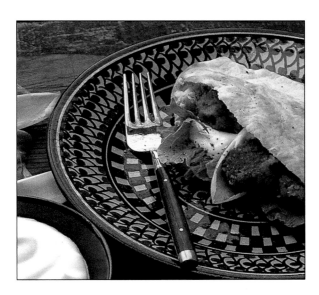

13

1 Put the chick-peas in a large bowl with enough cold water to cover. Leave to soak overnight.

2 Drain the chick-peas and put them in a saucepan. Add fresh water to cover, bring to the boil and boil rapidly for 10 minutes. Lower the heat and simmer for 1–1½ hours until the chick-peas are tender. Drain well.

3 Tip the chick-peas into a food processor. Add the chopped onion, garlic, fresh parsley, spices and baking powder, with salt and pepper to taste. Process to a firm paste.

4 Shape the mixture into walnut-size balls using your hands, and then flatten them slightly. Heat the oil for deep-frying in a large saucepan and fry the falafel

in batches until golden. Drain on kitchen paper and allow to cool completely. Wrap in several layers of foil for transporting to the picnic, and serve with pitta bread, salad and yogurt.

Pan Bagna

INGREDIENTS

1 extra-long French stick
150ml / ¼ pint / ⅔ cup French Dressing
1 small onion, thinly sliced
3 tomatoes, sliced
1 small green or red pepper, seeded and sliced
*50g / 2oz can anchovy fillets, drained
and halved*
*90g / 3½oz can tuna in oil, drained
and flaked*
50g / 2oz / ⅓ cup stoned black olives, halved

SERVES 4–6

1 Split the French stick horizontally along one side, without cutting all the way through the crust. Open the bread out and sprinkle the French dressing evenly over both cut surfaces.

2 Then arrange the onion, tomatoes, pepper, anchovies, tuna and olives on the bottom half of the stick. Re-form by pressing the halves firmly together.

3 Wrap the filled stick in clear film, lay a board on top and add several weights along the length of the sandwich (cans of fruit or vegetables work well). Leave for 1 hour so that the dressing soaks into the bread.

4 Remove the weights and board, then wrap the pan bagna in double foil for taking to the picnic. Cut into sections to serve.

Fennel & Lavender Tarts

INGREDIENTS

175g/6oz shortcrust pastry, thawed if frozen
FILLING
75g/3oz/6 tbsp butter
1 large Spanish onion, finely sliced
1 fennel bulb, trimmed and sliced
30ml/2 tbsp fresh lavender florets or 15ml/
1 tbsp dried culinary lavender, finely chopped
150ml/¼ pint/⅔ cup crème fraîche
2 egg yolks
salt and ground black pepper

SERVES 4

1 Roll out the pastry on a lightly floured surface and line four 7.5cm/3in loose-based individual flan tins. Prick the bottom of each pastry case with a fork and chill.

2 Preheat the oven to 200°C/400°F/ Gas 6. Make the filling. Melt the butter in a sauce-pan and soften the onion and fennel with the lavender over a low heat.

3 Line the pastry cases with greaseproof paper and bake blind for 5 minutes, then remove the paper and bake for 4 minutes more. Lower the oven temperature to 180°C/350°F/Gas 4.

4 Mix the crème fraîche and egg yolks in a jug and add salt and pepper to taste. Divide the onion mixture among the pastry cases, pour the crème fraîche mixture on top and bake for 10–15 minutes, until the filling has set. When cold, pack carefully in a rigid tub, adding a few extra lavender flowers, for garnishing.

15

Country-style Pork & Leek Pâté

INGREDIENTS

15g / ½oz / 1 tbsp butter
450g / 1lb leeks, trimmed and sliced
2–3 large garlic cloves, crushed
150g / 5oz rindless smoked streaky
bacon rashers
1kg / 2¼lb lean pork leg or shoulder, cubed
7.5ml / 1½ tsp chopped fresh thyme
3 fresh sage leaves, finely chopped
1.5ml / ¼ tsp ground cumin
1.5ml / ¼ tsp grated nutmeg
salt and ground black pepper
1 bay leaf, to garnish

SERVES 8–10

1 Preheat the oven to 180°C/350°F/ Gas 4. Melt the butter in a large frying pan. Add the leeks, cover and cook gently for 10 minutes. Stir in the garlic

and cook for 10 minutes more until the leeks are very soft. Set aside.

2 Reserve 2 bacon rashers. Grind the rest with the pork to a coarse purée by pulsing the mixture in small batches in a food processor. Scrape into a bowl and remove any white stringy bits. Add the leeks, herbs and spices to the bowl, with plenty of salt and pepper. Mix well.

3 Line a 1.5 litre/2½ pint/6¼ cup terrine with non-stick baking paper. Spoon in the pork mixture, pressing it down firmly into the corners. Tap the tin to settle the mixture, smooth the surface and arrange the reserved bacon and bay leaf on top. Cover tightly with foil.

4 Place the terrine in a roasting pan and pour in boiling water to come halfway up the sides. Bake in the oven for 1¼ hours, then carefully pour away the water. Leaving the terrine in the pan, place a board and weights (cans of fruit or vegetables work well) on top to compress the pâté as it cools. Chill in the fridge overnight, then remove the board and weights. Wrap the pâté carefully and transport to the picnic site in a chiller bag. Serve with large chunks of wholemeal bread.

Hummus with Tahini

INGREDIENTS

150g / 5oz / ¾ cup chick-peas
juice of 2 lemons
2 garlic cloves, sliced
30ml / 2 tbsp olive oil
pinch of cayenne pepper
150ml / ¼ pint / ⅔ cup tahini paste
extra olive oil and cayenne pepper, for sprinkling
salt and ground black pepper

SERVES 4–6

1 Put the chick-peas in a large bowl with enough cold water to cover. Leave them to soak overnight.

2 Drain the chick-peas and put them in a saucepan. Add fresh water to cover, bring to the boil and boil rapidly for 10 minutes. Lower the heat and simmer for 1–1½ hours until the chick-peas are tender. Drain well.

3 Tip the chick-peas into a food processor. Process to a smooth purée. Add the lemon juice, sliced garlic, olive oil, cayenne pepper and tahini paste. Process the mixture again until creamy, scraping down the sides of the bowl from time to time, as necessary.

4 Scrape the hummus into a plastic tub and add salt and pepper to taste. Seal the tub tightly and chill until ready to pack for the picnic. If possible, take along a little extra olive oil and cayenne pepper to sprinkle over the surface as a garnish. Hummus makes a delicious snack served with chilled crudités and pitta bread, or simply a couple of bright red radishes.

Potato & Onion Tortilla

INGREDIENTS

300ml / ½ pint / 1 ¼ cups olive oil
6 large potatoes, sliced
2 Spanish onions, sliced
6 size 2 eggs
salt and ground black pepper
cherry tomatoes, to serve

SERVES 4

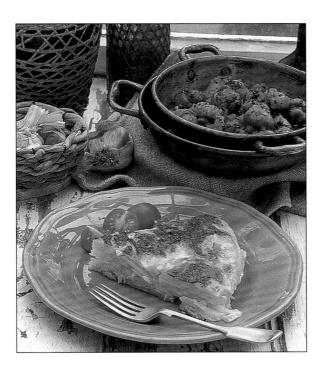

I Heat the oil in a large frying pan. Stir in the potatoes and onions. Sprinkle with a little salt, cover and cook over a gentle heat for 20 minutes until soft.

2 Beat the eggs in a large bowl. Using a slotted spoon, lift the potato and onion slices out of the pan and add to the eggs. Season to taste, then carefully pour off all but 60ml/4 tbsp of the oil remaining in the pan.

3 Then heat the oil again. Add the egg mixture and cook for 2–3 minutes until the base is set. Cover the pan with a plate and carefully invert the tortilla on to it.

Slide it back into the pan and cook for 5 minutes more, until it is golden brown on the outside and moist in the middle.

4 Cool, then wrap in foil and support in a box. Cut into wedges and serve with the cherry tomatoes.

Sun-dried Tomato Bread

INGREDIENTS

45ml/3 tbsp olive oil
1 large onion, finely chopped
400ml/14fl oz/1⅔ cups milk
15ml/1 tbsp tomato purée
675g/1½lb/6 cups strong plain flour
10ml/2 tsp salt
60ml/4 tbsp caster sugar
10g/¼oz sachet easy-blend dried yeast
75g/3oz/½ cup drained sun-dried tomatoes
in oil, chopped, plus 45ml/3 tbsp oil
from the jar

MAKES 4 SMALL LOAVES

1 Heat the olive oil in a small frying pan and fry the onion for 5 minutes over a gentle heat until softened. Set the pan aside. In a saucepan, heat the milk to hand-hot. Pour into a jug and stir in the tomato purée.

2 Sift the flour and salt into a mixing bowl. Stir in the sugar and yeast. Make a well in the centre and add the milk mixture, with the contents of the frying pan, the sun-dried tomatoes and their oil. Mix to a soft dough. Knead on a lightly floured surface for 10 minutes until smooth and elastic.

3 Lightly grease a baking sheet. Shape the dough into four rounds and place on the sheet, leaving plenty of room for rising. Cover with a dish towel and leave until the dough has doubled in bulk.

4 Preheat the oven to 220°C/425°F/Gas 7. Bake the loaves for 30 minutes, until they sound hollow when rapped on the bottom. Cool on a wire rack.

COOK'S TIP

The amount of liquid required to make the dough will depend on the absorbency of the flour. Add half the milk mixture at first, then add more as required.

20

Cheese & Chive Scones

INGREDIENTS

115g/4oz/1 cup self-raising white flour
115g/4oz/1 cup self-raising wholemeal flour
2.5ml/½ tsp salt
75g/3oz/½ cup feta cheese
15ml/1 tbsp finely snipped fresh chives
150ml/¼ pint/⅔ cup milk, plus extra for
glazing
1.5ml/¼ tsp cayenne pepper

MAKES 9

22

1 Preheat the oven to 200°C/400°F/Gas 6. Sift the flours and salt into a mixing bowl. Tip in any bran remaining in the sieve. Crumble in the feta cheese and rub it into the dry ingredients. Stir in the chives. Working quickly, mix in enough milk to make a soft dough. Knead the dough lightly.

2 Roll or pat out the dough on a floured surface to a thickness of about 2cm/¾in. Using a 6cm/ 2½in round cutter, cut out about 9 scones.

3 Transfer the scones to a non-stick baking sheet. Brush with milk, then sprinkle with cayenne pepper. Bake for 15 minutes, until golden brown. Allow the scones to cool on a wire rack, then pack in a tin. Serve with butter, or with a spread made by mixing cream cheese and finely snipped fresh chives.

Dill & Potato Cakes

INGREDIENTS

225g / 8oz / 2 cups self-raising flour
pinch of salt
40g / 1½oz / 3 tbsp butter, softened
15ml / 1 tbsp finely chopped fresh dill
175g / 6oz / 1 cup mashed potato, freshly made
30–45ml / 2–3 tbsp milk

MAKES 10

1 Preheat the oven to 230°C/450°F/ Gas 8. Grease a large baking sheet. Sift the flour and salt into a mixing bowl. Add the butter and dill. Mix in the mashed potato, with enough milk to make a soft, pliable dough.

2 Roll out the dough on a lightly floured surface. Cut into 10 neat rounds, using a 7.5cm/3in cutter. Place the rounds on the prepared baking sheet and bake for 25 minutes until risen and golden.

3 Allow the cakes to cool on a wire rack, then pack them in a tin. For a special picnic treat, serve with crème fraîche and smoked salmon.

VARIATION

Cheese & Herb Potato Cakes: Stir about 50g/2oz/½ cup crumbled blue cheese into the mashed potato mixture, and substitute fresh chives for the dill. Use 45ml/3 tbsp soured cream instead of the butter.

23

Salad Days

Tabbouleh with Fennel & Pomegranate

INGREDIENTS

225g/8oz/1⅓ cups bulgur wheat
2 fennel bulbs
1 small fresh red chilli, seeded and
finely chopped
1 celery stick, finely sliced
6–8 spring onions, chopped
90ml/6 tbsp chopped fresh mint
90ml/6 tbsp chopped fresh parsley
seeds from 1 pomegranate
30ml/2 tbsp olive oil
finely grated rind and juice of 2 lemons
salt and ground black pepper

SERVES 6

2 Cut the fennel bulbs in half and slice them both very thinly. Add to the bulgur, with the chilli, celery, spring onions, fresh herbs and pomegranate seeds. Pour over the olive oil, lemon rind and juice, add salt and pepper to taste and mix well.

3 Pack into a rigid tub for taking to the picnic. Serve with pitta bread and baby cos lettuce leaves. The salad needs to stand for at least 30 minutes before serving.

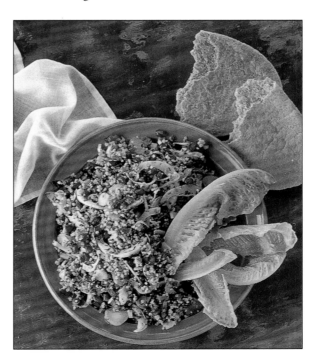

1 Place the bulgur wheat in a large bowl. Pour over cold water to cover. Leave to stand for 30 minutes, then tip into a sieve lined with muslin or a clean dish

towel. Drain well, then gather up the sides of the cloth and squeeze out as much liquid as possible from the bulgur. Tip it into a bowl.

Ratatouille

INGREDIENTS

2 aubergines (total weight about 450g/1lb)
60–75ml/4–5 tbsp olive oil
1 large onion, halved and sliced
2–3 garlic cloves, crushed
1 large red or yellow pepper, seeded and cut into thin strips
2 large courgettes, cut into 1cm/½in slices
675g/1½lb ripe tomatoes, peeled, seeded and chopped, or 475ml/16fl oz/2 cups passata
5ml/1 tsp herbes de Provence
salt and ground black pepper

SERVES 6

1 Preheat the grill. Cut the aubergines into 2cm/¾in slices. Brush both sides with olive oil and then grill until lightly browned, turning once. Cut the aubergine slices into cubes and set aside.

2 Heat 15ml/1 tbsp of the remaining oil in a flameproof casserole dish. Cook the onion over a medium heat for about 10 minutes until golden, stirring frequently. Add the garlic, pepper and courgettes. Cook for 10 minutes more.

3 Stir in the tomatoes or passata and aubergine cubes with the dried herbs. Add salt and pepper to taste and simmer gently, covered, for about 20 minutes. Stir the mixture occasionally.

4 Remove the lid and cook for 20 minutes more or until all the vegetables are tender and the cooking liquid has thickened. Tip into a bowl and cool quickly, then pack in a plastic tub. Serve at room temperature with plenty of bread to mop up the delicious juices. Cornets of pepper salami would be good with this picnic salad.

French Bean Salad

INGREDIENTS

175g/6oz cherry tomatoes, halved
5ml/1 tsp granulated sugar
450g/1lb French beans, trimmed
175g/6oz feta cheese, cut in small wedges
salt and ground black pepper
DRESSING
45ml/3 tbsp white wine vinegar
1.5ml/¼ tsp Dijon mustard
2 garlic cloves, crushed
90ml/6 tbsp olive oil

SERVES 6

1 Preheat the oven to 230°C/450°F/Gas 8. Put the cherry tomatoes on a baking sheet with the cut sides up. Sprinkle over the sugar and add salt and pepper to taste. Bake the tomatoes in the preheated oven for about 20 minutes, then leave them to cool.

2 Bring a saucepan of lightly salted water to the boil. Add the French beans and cook for about 10 minutes. Meanwhile, make the dressing. Mix the white wine vinegar, mustard and garlic in a bowl. Gradually whisk in the oil and add salt and pepper to taste.

3 Drain the cooked beans, tip them into a bowl and immediately pour over the dressing. Toss well to ensure the dressing is evenly distributed.

4 When the beans have cooled, stir in the roasted cherry tomatoes and the wedges of feta cheese. Pack the salad in a sealed plastic tub and keep in the fridge before transporting to the picnic site in a chiller bag.

Potato Salad with Sausage

INGREDIENTS

450g/1lb small waxy potatoes
30–45ml/2–3 tbsp dry white wine
2 shallots, finely chopped
15ml/1 tbsp chopped fresh parsley
15ml/1 tbsp chopped fresh tarragon
175g/6oz cooked garlic sausage,
such as kielbasa, sliced
parsley sprig, to garnish
DRESSING
15ml/1 tbsp tarragon vinegar
10ml/2 tsp Dijon mustard
75ml/5 tbsp olive oil
salt and ground black pepper

SERVES 4

1 Put the potatoes in a saucepan with lightly salted cold water to cover. Bring to the boil, lower the heat and simmer for 10–15 minutes until they are tender.

2 Drain the potatoes, refresh them under cold running water and drain again. Peel the potatoes if you prefer, or leave in their skins. Cut into 5mm/¼in slices, place in a bowl and sprinkle with the wine and shallots.

3 Make the dressing. Mix the vinegar and mustard in a bowl. Gradually whisk in the oil, and season to taste. Pour the dressing over the potato mixture.

4 Then sprinkle the chopped parsley and tarragon over the salad, and add the sausage slices. Toss lightly to mix. Season with salt and pepper. Pack in a plastic tub and serve at room temperature, garnished with a fresh parsley sprig.

VARIATION

If preferred, leave out the sausage and serve the potato salad as it is, with rollmop herrings.

28

Frisée Salad with Bacon

INGREDIENTS

1 frisée lettuce, separated into leaves
45ml/3 tbsp extra-virgin olive oil
175g/6oz piece of smoked bacon, diced
1 thick slice of white bread, crust removed, diced
DRESSING
1 garlic clove, bruised
15ml/1 tbsp red wine vinegar
10ml/2 tsp Dijon mustard
45ml/3 tbsp olive oil
salt and ground black pepper

SERVES 4

1 Tear the lettuce leaves into bite-size pieces and place in a bowl. Wash, dry and store in a plastic bag in the salad compartment of the fridge.

2 Heat 15ml/1 tbsp of the oil in a frying pan. Add the bacon and fry over a medium heat until well browned, stirring occasionally. Using a slotted spoon, lift out the bacon pieces and drain on kitchen paper.

3 Add a further 30ml/2 tbsp oil to the pan. When hot, fry the bread cubes, turning frequently, until evenly browned. Remove the croûtons with a slotted spoon and drain them on kitchen paper. When cold, pack the croûtons and bacon in separate plastic tubs.

4 Make the dressing. Mix the garlic, vinegar, mustard and oil in a leakproof beaker. Season with salt and pepper to taste.

5 Pack the lettuce, bacon, croûtons and dressing separately. When ready to serve, tip the lettuce into a salad bowl and add the bacon and croûtons. Shake the dressing well and pour it over the salad. Toss quickly, making sure the salad leaves are evenly covered, and serve.

COOK'S TIP

For serving at home, make this a warm salad. Fry the croûtons first, then the bacon cubes. Drain them on kitchen paper. Add the garlic, vinegar, mustard and remaining oil to the frying pan. Whisk over the heat until warm, then pour over the lettuce and toss lightly. To serve, sprinkle the lettuce with the fried bacon and croûtons.

30

Spanish Potatoes

INGREDIENTS

675g / 1½lb small new potatoes
2 garlic cloves, sliced
1 small dried red chilli, crumbled
2.5ml / ½ tsp ground cumin
10ml / 2 tsp mild paprika
30ml / 2 tbsp red wine vinegar
75ml / 5 tbsp olive oil
1 red or green pepper, seeded and sliced
coarse sea salt to serve

SERVES 4

1 Put the potatoes in a saucepan with lightly salted cold water to cover. Bring to the boil, lower the heat and simmer for 15 minutes until they are tender.

2 Drain the potatoes, refresh them under cold running water and drain again. Peel the potatoes if you prefer, or leave in their skins. Cut into chunks.

3 Put the sliced garlic and chilli in a mortar. Crush with a pestle, then add the ground cumin, paprika and red wine vinegar and mix to form a paste.

4 Heat the oil in a large frying pan and fry the potatoes until golden, turning them often. Add the pepper slices and cook for 1 minute, then stir in the garlic paste. Cook, stirring, for 2 minutes. Tip the spiced potatoes into a bowl and leave to cool. Cover the bowl securely for packing and grind sea salt over the potatoes just before serving.

Swiss Cheese Salad

INGREDIENTS

2 skinless, boneless chicken breasts
300ml/½ pint/1¼ cups chicken stock
225g/8oz Gruyère cheese
225g/8oz thickly sliced cooked ham
or ox tongue
1 lollo rosso lettuce
1 butterhead lettuce
1 bunch watercress
3 celery sticks, sliced
60ml/4 tbsp sesame seeds, toasted
2 green-skinned eating apples
DRESSING
75ml/5 tbsp sunflower oil
5ml/1 tsp sesame oil
45ml/3 tbsp lemon juice
10ml/2 tsp chopped fresh mint
3 drops of Tabasco sauce

SERVES 4

1 Put the chicken breasts in a saucepan. Pour over the stock and bring to simmering point. Simmer for 15 minutes or until the chicken is just cooked. Drain, reserving the stock for another recipe. Cool the chicken quickly.

2 Make the dressing by mixing all the ingredients in a leakproof beaker. Cut the chicken, cheese and ham or tongue into fine strips. Put in a tub, moisten with a little of the dressing and chill in the fridge until required.

3 Wash and dry the salad leaves. Pack them, with the celery, in a loosely-closed plastic bag in a chiller box. Add the tub of cheese and cold meat strips and pack the sesame seeds and apples separately, with the dressing. Dress the leaves and assemble the salad on individual plates at the picnic site, slicing the apple and adding it at the last minute.

Stuffed Peppers

INGREDIENTS

6 even-size peppers, any colour
60ml/4 tbsp olive oil, plus extra for drizzling
1 large onion, finely chopped
3 drained canned anchovy fillets, chopped
2 garlic cloves, crushed
3 tomatoes, peeled and diced
60ml/4 tbsp white wine
450g/1lb/4 cups cooked rice (about
200g/7oz/1 cup raw weight)
45ml/3 tbsp finely chopped fresh parsley
115g/4oz/⅔ cup diced mozzarella cheese
90ml/6 tbsp grated Parmesan cheese
salt and ground black pepper
flat-leaf parsley, to garnish

SERVES 6

34

1 Preheat the oven to 190°C/375°F/Gas 5. Cut the tops off the peppers and remove the cores and seeds. Trim the bottoms, if necessary, so that they stand level. Bring a saucepan of lightly salted water to the boil, add the peppers and blanch for 3–4 minutes. Lift out with a slotted spoon and dry inside and out with kitchen paper.

2 Heat the olive oil in a large frying pan and fry the chopped onion for about 5 minutes, until softened. Stir in the chopped anchovy fillets, garlic, tomatoes and white wine. Cook, stirring occasionally, for 5 minutes.

3 Off the heat, stir the cooked rice, fresh parsley, mozzarella and two-thirds of the Parmesan into the onion mixture. Season with salt and pepper to taste. Sprinkle the pepper cavities with salt and pepper, then stuff with the filling.

4 Stand the peppers upright in a shallow baking dish that will just hold them comfortably. Top with the remaining Parmesan and drizzle with a little olive oil. Pour in enough water to come 1cm/½in up the sides of the peppers.

5 Bake the peppers in the preheated oven for about 25 minutes, then allow them to cool to room temperature. Transport the peppers to the picnic site in the dish in which they were baked, using balls of crumpled foil to keep them upright. Garnish each of the peppers with a sprig of flat-leaf parsley before serving.

Main Attractions

Chicken & Apricot Filo Pie

INGREDIENTS

75g/3oz/½ cup bulgur wheat
120ml/4fl oz/½ cup boiling water
75g/3oz/6 tbsp butter
1 onion, chopped
450g/1lb/2 cups minced chicken
50g/2oz/¼ cup ready-to-eat dried apricots,
finely chopped
25g/1oz/¼ cup blanched almonds, chopped
5ml/1 tsp ground cinnamon
2.5ml/½ tsp ground allspice
60ml/4 tbsp Greek yogurt
15ml/1 tbsp snipped fresh chives
30ml/2 tbsp chopped fresh parsley
6 large sheets of filo pastry
salt and ground black pepper, to taste
halved fresh chives, to garnish

SERVES 6

1 Preheat the oven to 200°C/400°F/Gas 6. Soak the bulgur wheat in boiling water for 10 minutes, until the water is absorbed. Drain and squeeze dry.

2 Heat 25g/1oz/2 tbsp of the butter in a frying pan. Fry the onion and chicken gently until golden. Stir in the apricots, almonds and bulgur wheat; cook for 2 minutes more. Off the heat, stir in the spices, yogurt, fresh herbs and seasoning.

3 Melt the remaining butter. Cut the filo into 25cm/10in rounds. Layer three rounds in a 23cm/9in loose-based flan tin, brushing each of the layers with melted butter. Spoon in the chicken mixture, then crumple the remaining filo rounds, brush each one with butter, and place them on top of the pie.

4 Brush over any remaining butter and bake for about 30 minutes, until the crust is golden and crisp. When the tin has cooled, pack it carefully in a rigid box (filo is fragile). Serve the pie in wedges, garnished with fresh chives.

37

Stuffed Turkey Breast with Lemon

INGREDIENTS

675g/1½lb turkey breast, in one piece
1 carrot, cut into matchsticks
1 courgette, cut into matchsticks
75g/3oz cooked ham, cut into matchsticks
2 thick slices of white bread, crusts removed,
soaked in a little milk to soften
10 stoned green olives, finely chopped
1 large garlic clove, crushed
60ml/4 tbsp chopped fresh parsley
60ml/4 tbsp finely shredded fresh basil
1 egg, lightly beaten
1.5ml/¼ tsp grated lemon rind
30ml/2 tbsp grated Parmesan cheese
60ml/4 tbsp olive oil
250ml/8fl oz/1 cup warm chicken stock
½ lemon, cut in thin wedges
salt and ground black pepper

SERVES 4–5

1 Remove any bones, skin or fat from the turkey. Cut part of the way through the breast so that the halves can be opened out like a book. Pound the meat to obtain one large piece of even thickness.

2 Preheat the oven to 200°C/400°F/Gas 6. Blanch the carrot and courgette sticks in a pan of boiling water for 2 minutes. Then drain and mix with the ham.

3 Squeeze the bread dry, place it in a mixing bowl and break it up with a fork. Add the olives, garlic, herbs, egg, lemon rind and Parmesan cheese. Season with salt and pepper and mix well.

4 Then spread the bread mixture over the meat, leaving a narrow border around the out-side. Arrange the vegetable and ham matchsticks on top, then roll the turkey up and tie it with a piece of string.

5 Heat the olive oil in a flameproof casserole dish and brown the turkey roll. Add the stock and lemon wedges, cover the dish and bake in the oven for 15 minutes. Remove the lid and the lemon wedges. Bake, uncovered, for 30 minutes more until the roll is fully cooked, basting occasionally. Cool quickly. Wrap the turkey roll in double foil and slice at the picnic site. Serve solo with green salad or with a lemon mayonnaise.

Cod Plaki

INGREDIENTS

300ml / ½ pint / 1¼ cups olive oil
2 onions, thinly sliced
3 beefsteak tomatoes, roughly chopped
3 garlic cloves, thinly sliced
5ml / 1 tsp granulated sugar
5ml / 1 tsp chopped fresh dill
5ml / 1 tsp chopped fresh mint
5ml / 1 tsp chopped fresh celery leaves
15ml / 1 tbsp chopped fresh parsley
300ml / ½ pint / 1¼ cups water
6 cod steaks
juice of 1 lemon
salt and ground black pepper
fresh herbs, to garnish

SERVES 6

2 Place the fish steaks on top of the mixture and cook gently for 10–12 minutes or until the fish is just cooked. Pour over the lemon juice. Lift out the

cod steaks with a slotted spoon and arrange them in a picnic dish. Spoon the sauce over and cool quickly. Cover the dish tightly and pack in a chiller bag. Garnish with fresh herbs to serve.

1 Heat the oil in a frying pan and fry the onions until golden. Add the tomatoes, garlic, sugar and chopped herbs. Cook for 2 minutes more, then pour over the

water. Add seasoning and simmer for 25 minutes or until the liquid has reduced by one-third.

Sweet Potato Roulade

INGREDIENTS

450g / 1lb sweet potatoes, freshly boiled
12 allspice berries, crushed
4 eggs, separated
50g / 2oz / ½ cup grated Edam or
Cheddar cheese
salt and ground black pepper
15ml / 1 tbsp sesame seeds
FILLING
225g / 8oz / 1 cup low-fat soft cheese
75ml / 5 tbsp natural yogurt
6–8 spring onions, thinly sliced
30ml / 2 tbsp chopped Brazil nuts, roasted

SERVES 6

1 Preheat the oven to 200°C/400°F/Gas 6. Grease a 33 x 25cm/13 x 10in Swiss roll tin and line with non-stick baking paper. Make the filling by mixing the soft cheese, yogurt, spring onions and nuts in a bowl. Cover the mixture and keep in the fridge until required.

2 Chop the sweet potato roughly and put it in a food processor with the allspice. Pulse until just smooth, then spoon into a bowl and stir in the egg yolks and cheese, with salt and pepper to taste.

3 Whisk the egg whites to stiff peaks. Lightly stir one-third of the whites into the sweet potato mixture to lighten it, then fold in the rest. Spoon the mixture into the prepared tin, level the surface and bake for 10–15 minutes until firm to the touch.

4 Have ready a sheet of non-stick baking paper on a clean dish towel. Sprinkle the paper with the sesame seeds, then carefully invert the cooked sponge on to it. Trim the edges, roll the sponge up and leave to cool. Unroll, spread with the filling and roll up again. Pack in a rigid box and slice at the picnic site. Serve with salad leaves.

41

Mediterranean Quiche

INGREDIENTS

225g/8oz/2 cups plain flour
pinch of salt
pinch of mustard powder
115g/4oz/½ cup chilled butter, cubed
50g/2oz/½ cup grated Gruyère cheese
30ml/2 tbsp mild French mustard
FILLING
50g/2oz can anchovies, drained
60ml/4 tbsp milk
45ml/3 tbsp olive oil
2 large Spanish onions, sliced
1 red pepper, seeded and sliced
3 egg yolks
350ml/12fl oz/1½ cups double cream
1 garlic clove, crushed
*175g/6oz/1½ cups grated mature
Cheddar cheese*
2 large tomatoes, thickly sliced
salt and ground black pepper
shredded fresh basil, to garnish

SERVES 10–12

1 Mix the flour, salt and mustard powder in a food processor. Add the butter and pulse the mixture until it resembles breadcrumbs. Add the cheese and process briefly. With the motor running, add iced water until the mixture forms a ball. Wrap the dough in clear film and chill for 30 minutes.

2 Preheat the oven to 200°C/400°F/Gas 6. Make the filling. Soak the anchovies in the milk for 20 minutes. Heat the oil in a frying pan and fry the onions and red pepper until soft. In a bowl, beat the egg yolks, cream, garlic and Cheddar cheese with plenty of salt and pepper.

3 Roll out the pastry on a lightly floured surface and line a 23cm/ 9in loose-based flan tin. Spread the mustard over the pastry case. Arrange the toma- toes in a layer on the bottom, add the onion mixture, and drain and arrange the anchovies on top.

4 Pour over the egg mixture and bake for 20–25 minutes. Lower the oven temperature to 180°C/ 350°F/Gas 4 and bake for 25 minutes more. Cool, wrap the tin in foil and pack it in a rigid box. Serve the quiche in slices, garnished with the fresh basil.

Broccoli & Chestnut Terrine

INGREDIENTS

450g/1lb broccoli, cut into small florets
225g/8oz cooked chestnuts, roughly chopped
50g/2oz/1 cup fresh wholemeal breadcrumbs
60ml/4 tbsp natural yogurt
30ml/2 tbsp grated Parmesan cheese
2 eggs, beaten
salt and ground black pepper

SERVES 4–6

44

1 Preheat the oven to 180°C/350°F/Gas 4. Line a 900g/2lb loaf tin with non-stick baking paper. Blanch or steam the broccoli for 3–4 minutes until just tender. Drain well. Set aside about a quarter of the smallest florets and chop the rest finely.

2 In a large bowl, mix the chopped chestnuts, breadcrumbs, natural yogurt and Parmesan cheese. Stir in salt and pepper to taste, then fold in the chopped broccoli florets and beaten eggs.

3 Gently fold the reserved florets into the mixture. Spoon into the prepared loaf tin and level the surface with the back of a wooden spoon.

4 Place the tin in a roasting pan and pour in boiling water to come halfway up the sides of the tin. Bake for 25 minutes. Cool quickly, wrap the tin in foil and pack it in a box. At the picnic site, turn it out on to a board. Cut into slices and serve with salad leaves and cold new potatoes, if liked.

COOK'S TIP

For an unbeatable taste sensation, serve the terrine with Spanish Potatoes and fresh cherry tomatoes.

Country Pie

INGREDIENTS

900g/2lb puff pastry, thawed if frozen
beaten egg, to glaze
FILLING
1 small duck
1 small chicken
350g/12oz pork belly, minced
1 egg, lightly beaten
2 shallots, finely chopped
2.5ml/½ tsp ground cinnamon
2.5ml/½ tsp grated nutmeg
5ml/1 tsp Worcestershire sauce
finely grated rind of 1 lemon
salt and ground black pepper
175ml/6fl oz/¾ cup red wine
600ml/1 pint/2½ cups well-flavoured stock
15g/½ oz/1 tbsp gelatine
HOT WATER PASTRY
675g/1½lb/6 cups plain flour
225g/8 oz hard white fat, cubed
300ml/½ pint/1¼ cups water
beaten egg, to glaze

SERVES 12

1 Make the filling. Dice the poultry breasts and set them aside. Trim the carcasses, and mix the meat with the pork. Add the beaten egg, shallots, spices, Worcestershire sauce and lemon rind. Season well. Pour over all but 15ml/1 tbsp of wine. Marinate for 15 minutes.

2 Make the pastry. Sift the flour into a bowl. Bring the fat and water to the boil, pour it on to the flour and mix quickly to a dough. Cool slightly, then knead. Keep warm, covered with a cloth.

3 Preheat the oven to 200°C/400°F/Gas 6. Roll out the pastry on a lightly floured surface. Use two-thirds of the pastry to line a greased 25cm/10in cake tin; allow a little pastry to hang over the top. Fill with alternate layers of pork mixture and diced poultry and ham. Make a lid with the remaining pastry and seal well. Cut two large holes in the lid and add pastry decorations.

4 Bake for 20 minutes, glaze with egg and lower the oven temperature to 180°C/350°F/Gas 4. Cover the pie with foil and bake for 1 hour more.

5 Degrease the stock. Pour the stock into a pan, heat and whisk in the gelatine until no lumps are left. Insert a funnel in the pie and pour in the stock. Chill the pie in the fridge for 24 hours, before wrapping and packing. Cut the pie into thick wedges to serve.

Wild Mushroom Pie

INGREDIENTS

450g / 1lb puff pastry, thawed if frozen
beaten egg, to glaze
FILLING
150g / 5oz / 2/3 cup butter
2 shallots, finely chopped
2 garlic cloves, crushed
450g / 1lb / 4 cups mixed wild mushrooms,
sliced
45ml / 3 tbsp chopped fresh parsley
30ml / 2 tbsp double cream
salt and ground black pepper

SERVES 6

1 Make the filling. Melt 50g/2oz/¼ cup of the butter in a large saucepan. Gently fry the chopped shallots and crushed garlic cloves over a low heat for about 5 minutes, until softened but not browned.

2 Then add the remaining butter to the pan. When it has melted, stir in the mushrooms and cook over a low heat for 35–40 minutes. Pour off the excess liquid and stir in the chopped parsley and double cream, adding salt and ground black pepper to taste. Allow the mixture to cool.

3 Preheat the oven to 220°C/425°F/Gas 7. Roll out half the pastry on a lightly floured surface. Using a plate as a guide, cut out a 23cm/9in round. Place the round on a baking sheet and pile the filling in the centre. Roll out the rest of the pastry and cut a slightly larger round, to cover the base and filling. Lop the pastry over the rolling pin and lay it over the filling, then firmly press the pastry edges together to seal.

4 Brush the top of the pie with beaten egg to glaze and decorate with pastry trimmings. Cut three holes in the top of the crust. Bake in the oven for 45 minutes or until the pastry has risen and is golden. Turn out the pie on to a wire rack and allow to cool completely, then wrap the pie in foil and transport to the picnic site in a rigid box. Cut the pie into thick wedges to serve.

Sweet Treats

Apple Crumble Cake

INGREDIENTS

CRUMBLE TOPPING
75g/3oz/¾ cup self-raising flour
2.5ml/½ tsp ground cinnamon
40g/1½oz/3 tbsp butter
25g/1oz/2 tbsp caster sugar
FRUIT BASE
50g/2oz/4 tbsp butter, softened
75g/3oz/6 tbsp caster sugar
1 size 3 egg, beaten
115g/4oz/1 cup self-raising flour, sifted
2 cooking apples, peeled, cored and sliced
50g/2oz/⅓ cup sultanas

SERVES 8–10

1 Preheat the oven to 180°C/350°F/Gas 4. Grease a deep 18cm/7 inch springform tin, line the base with greaseproof paper and grease the paper.

2 Make the topping. Sift the flour and cinnamon into a large mixing bowl. Rub the butter into the flour until it resembles breadcrumbs, then stir in the sugar. Set aside.

3 Make the fruit base. Place the butter, sugar, egg and flour in a bowl and beat for 1–2 minutes until smooth. Spoon into the prepared tin.

4 Mix together the apple slices and sultanas and spread them evenly over the top. Sprinkle with the topping. Bake in the centre of the oven for about 1 hour. Cool in the tin for 10 minutes before turning out on to a wire rack and peeling off the lining paper.

5 Decorate the cake with slices of red dessert apple and sprinkle with caster sugar and a pinch of ground cinnamon. Transport the cake to the picnic in a tin. Serve in thick slices with cream, if liked.

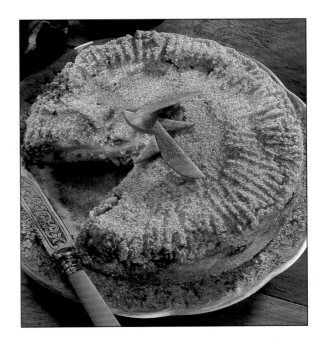

Savarin with Summer Fruit

INGREDIENTS

115g/4oz/½ cup butter, softened
275g/10oz/2½ cups plain flour
10g/¼oz sachet easy-blend dried yeast
60ml/4 tbsp caster sugar
4 eggs, beaten
60ml/4 tbsp hand-hot water
5ml/1 tsp vanilla essence
450g/1lb fresh raspberries or
strawberries, hulled
mint leaves, to decorate
clotted cream, to serve
SYRUP
225g/8oz/1 cup caster sugar
600ml/1 pint/2½ cups water
90ml/6 tbsp redcurrant jelly
45ml/3 tbsp Kirsch (optional)

SERVES 4–6

1 Using 15ml/1 tbsp of the butter, generously grease a 23cm/9in ring mould. Put the flour, yeast and sugar in a food processor and pulse to mix. With the motor running, add the beaten eggs, water and vanilla essence through the feeder tube. Process to a soft dough, scraping down the sides of the processor as needed, then add the remaining butter and pulse about 10 times to incorporate it.

2 Place the dough in evenly spaced spoonfuls around the ring mould. Cover the mould and leave the dough to rise until it has doubled in bulk. Preheat the oven to 200°C/400°F/Gas 6.

3 Place the ring mould in the oven and immediately turn the heat down to 180°C/350°F/Gas 4. Bake for 25 minutes until golden brown and springy to the touch. Cool on a wire rack.

4 Make the syrup by heating the sugar, water and two-thirds of the redcurrant jelly in a pan. Stir until smooth, then boil for 3 minutes. Cool slightly, then add the Kirsch, if using. Stir 30ml/2 tbsp of the syrup into the reserved redcurrant jelly until dissolved, to make a glaze. Set aside.

5 Place the warm cake on a wire rack over a baking tray. Spoon the syrup over repeatedly until absorbed, then carefully place the cake in a shallow serving dish and pour over any remaining syrup. Brush the redcurrant glaze over the top. Cover and transport very carefully. Pack the berries, cream and mint leaves separately. At the picnic, fill the centre with berries. Decorate, then serve with cream.

52

Raspberry Crumble Muffins

INGREDIENTS

175g/6oz/1½ cups plain flour
10ml/2 tsp baking powder
pinch of salt
50g/2oz/¼ cup caster sugar
50g/2oz/¼ cup soft light brown sugar
5ml/1 tsp ground cinnamon
115g/4oz/½ cup butter, melted
1 egg, beaten
120ml/4fl oz/½ cup milk
150g/5oz/scant 1 cup raspberries
grated rind of 1 lemon
CRUMBLE TOPPING
25g/1oz/3 tbsp pecan nuts or walnuts,
finely chopped
50g/2oz/¼ cup soft dark brown sugar
45ml/3 tbsp plain flour
5ml/1 tsp ground cinnamon
40g/1½oz/3 tbsp butter, melted

MAKES 12

1 Preheat the oven to 180°C/350°F/Gas 4. Lightly grease a 12-cup muffin tin, or use paper cases. Sift the flour, baking powder and salt into a bowl. Stir in the sugars and cinnamon.

2 Make a well in the centre. Add the butter, egg and milk and mix until just combined. Stir in the raspberries and lemon rind. Divide the mixture among the muffin cups.

3 Make the crumble topping by mixing the nuts, dark brown sugar, flour and cinnamon in a bowl. Add the melted butter and stir to blend. Spoon some of the crumble over each uncooked muffin. Bake in the oven for 20–25 minutes, or until the muffins are well risen and golden brown. Allow to cool on a wire rack, then pack in a tin.

54

Dried Fruit Tea Bread

INGREDIENTS

170g/6oz/1 cup dried fruit, roughly chopped
250 ml/8fl oz/1 cup hot tea
225g/8oz/2 cups wholemeal self-raising
flour
5ml/1 tsp grated nutmeg
50g/2oz/¼ cup dark muscovado sugar
45ml/3 tbsp sunflower oil
45ml/3 tbsp skimmed milk
demerara sugar, for sprinkling

SERVES 8–10

1 Soak the chopped dried fruit in the hot tea for several hours or overnight, making sure the fruit is completely covered. Drain and reserve both the fruit and the liquid.

3 Sift the flour into a large bowl with the grated nutmeg. Stir in the muscovado sugar, fruit and tea. Add the sunflower oil and skimmed milk and mix well.

2 Preheat the oven to 180°C/350°F/Gas 4. Grease a 7in/18cm round cake tin and line the base with non-stick baking paper. Take care to grease the paper well.

4 Spoon the mixture into the prepared tin and sprinkle with demerara sugar. Bake for 50–55 minutes or until the mixture is just firm. Cool on a wire rack then cut into thick chunks and pack in a tin.

Biscotti

INGREDIENTS

50g/2oz/¼ cup unsalted butter, softened
115g/4oz/½ cup caster sugar
175g/6oz/1½ cups self-raising flour
1.5ml/¼ tsp salt
10ml/2 tsp baking powder
5ml/1 tsp ground coriander
finely grated rind of 1 lemon
50g/2oz/¼ cup polenta
1 egg, lightly beaten
10ml/2 tsp brandy or orange liqueur
50g/2oz/¼ cup pistachio nuts

MAKES 24

1 Preheat the oven to 160°C/325°F/Gas 3. Lightly grease a baking sheet. In a mixing bowl, cream the butter with the sugar until the mixture is light and fluffy.

2 Sift the flour, salt, baking powder and coriander into the mixing bowl. Add the lemon rind, polenta, egg and brandy or liqueur. Mix to a soft dough.

3 Work in the nuts until they are evenly distributed. Halve the mixture and then shape each half into a long sausage, about 23cm/9in long and 6cm/ 2½in wide. Place on the baking sheet and bake for about 30 minutes until risen and just firm. Remove the baking sheet, but leave the oven on.

4 When the loaves are cool, use a serrated knife to cut each of them diagonally into 12 thin slices. Place the slices on the baking sheet, cut-side up, and bake for 10 minutes more, until crisp. Cool on a wire rack, then pack in a tin.

COOK'S TIP

These Italian biscuits are traditionally served dipped in a sweet dessert wine – ideal for those who don't have to drive home from the picnic.

Figs with Ricotta Cream

INGREDIENTS

115g/4oz/½ cup ricotta cheese
45ml/3 tbsp crème fraîche
15ml/1 tbsp clear honey
2.5ml/½ tsp vanilla essence
4 ripe, fresh figs
grated nutmeg, to decorate

SERVES 4

1 Mix the ricotta cheese, crème fraîche, honey and vanilla essence in a bowl. Transfer to a tub with a tight-fitting lid and pack in a chiller bag with the figs. Pack a nutmeg – and a nutmeg grater – if you really want to impress.

2 When ready to serve, trim the stalks from the figs. Make four cuts through each fig from the stalk end, cutting them almost through, but leaving them joined at the base. Place each fig on an individual plate and open it out like a flower.

3 Spoon a little ricotta cream on to each plate and grate nutmeg on top to serve.

VARIATION
Use low-fat cream cheese instead of ricotta, if you prefer, and substitute Greek yogurt for the crème fraîche. Sprinkle the yogurt with demerara sugar.

Chocolate Chip Banana Crêpes

INGREDIENTS

2 ripe bananas
200ml/7fl oz/scant 1 cup milk
2 eggs
150g/5oz/1¼ cups self-raising flour
40g/1½oz/⅓ cup ground almonds
15ml/1 tbsp caster sugar
45ml/3 tbsp plain chocolate chips
butter for frying
TOPPING
150ml/¼ pint/⅔ cup double cream
15ml/1 tbsp icing sugar
toasted flaked almonds

MAKES 16

1 Mash the bananas in a bowl with a fork. Stir in half the milk, then beat in the eggs. Gradually beat in the flour, ground almonds and caster sugar. Make a well in the centre of the mixture and pour in the remaining milk. Add the chocolate chips and stir to make a thick batter.

2 Heat a knob of butter in a non-stick frying pan. Spoon in a little of the batter, so that it spreads to form a small crêpe. Make more crêpes in the same way, but do not overcrowd the pan.

3 When bubbles appear on the top of the crêpes, turn them over and briefly cook the other side. Cool on a wire rack, then pack into a tin.

4 For the topping, either whip the cream with the icing sugar and pack in a sealed tub in a chiller bag, or cheat and use aerosol cream. Pack the toasted flaked almonds separately, to decorate the crêpes.

59

COOK'S TIP
The easiest way to cook these is in an electric frying pan, if you have one. Children enjoy making them (with adult help), especially if they are allowed to use the chocolate chips to make faces on the crêpes.

Orange-blossom Jelly

INGREDIENTS

75ml/5 tbsp caster sugar
150ml/¼ pint/⅔ cup water
30ml/2 tbsp powdered gelatine
600ml/1 pint/2½ cups freshly squeezed
orange juice
30ml/2 tbsp orange-flower water

SERVES 4–6

I Place the caster sugar and water in a small saucepan. Heat gently, stirring occasionally, until the sugar has dissolved. Tip into a heatproof bowl and sprinkle in the gelatine. Leave to stand until the gelatine has absorbed the liquid and is solid.

2 Melt the gelatine again, by placing the bowl over a pan of gently simmering water. When it is clear, remove it from the heat. Leave the gelatine to cool, but do not let it solidify. Stir it into the orange juice and add the orange-flower water.

3 Then wet a jelly mould, pour in the orange jelly and chill in the fridge for at least 3 hours until solidly set. Turn the jelly out by immersing the mould in a bowl of hot water. Return the jelly to the mould and wrap it carefully in a chiller bag to transport to the picnic. Turn the jelly out to serve; for a special occasion, decorate with fresh flowers. Serve with dessert biscuits such as langues de chat, if you like.

COOK'S TIP

The acid in orange juice inhibits the setting action of gelatine, which is why the quantity in this recipe is relatively high. It is important to cool the liquid gelatine before adding it to the orange juice, or it will form threads.

Lemon Tart

INGREDIENTS

*350g/12oz shortcrust or sweet
shortcrust pastry
grated rind of 2 large lemons
150ml/¼ pint/⅔ cup freshly squeezed
lemon juice
115g/4oz/½ cup caster sugar
60ml/4 tbsp crème fraîche or double cream
4 eggs, plus 3 egg yolks
icing sugar, for dusting*

SERVES 8–10

62

1 Preheat the oven to 190°C/375°F/ Gas 5. Roll out the pastry on a lightly floured surface and line a 23cm/9in flan tin. Prick the base of the pastry, line with foil and baking beans and bake blind for 15 minutes. Remove the foil and beans and return the pastry case to the oven to cook for a further 5–7 minutes, until golden.

2 Whisk the lemon rind, juice and sugar in a bowl until light and fluffy. Gradually whisk in the crème fraîche or double cream, then add the whole eggs one at a time, whisking after each addition. Then whisk in the egg yolks.

3 Pour the filling into the pastry case and bake in the oven for 15–20 minutes, until set. Leave to cool and then pack the tart, still supported by the tin, in a rigid box. Transfer the tart to a plate at the picnic site and dust with icing sugar to serve.

Pear & Almond Cream Tart

INGREDIENTS

*350g/12oz shortcrust or sweet
shortcrust pastry
3 firm pears
lemon juice
15ml/1 tbsp peach brandy or water
60ml/4 tbsp peach preserve, strained
ALMOND CREAM FILLING
65g/2½oz/5 tbsp butter
60ml/4 tbsp caster sugar
75g/3oz/¾ cup ground almonds
1 egg, plus 1 egg white
few drops of almond essence*

SERVES 6

1 Preheat the oven to 190°C/375°F/Gas 5. Roll out the pastry on a lightly floured surface and line a 23cm/9in flan tin. Make the almond cream filling by creaming the butter with the sugar in a small bowl, then stirring in the ground almonds, egg, egg white and almond essence.

2 Peel the pears, cut them in half and remove the cores. Brush with lemon juice to stop them from going brown. With the rounded sides up, slice the pears thinly crossways, keeping the slices together.

3 Spoon the almond cream filling into the uncooked pastry case. Slide a palette knife under each pear in turn, gently pressing the top to fan out the slices, and transfer it to the pastry case. Arrange the pears like the spokes of a wheel. Bake the tart in the oven for 50–55 minutes or until the filling is set and golden brown. Cool on a wire rack.

4 Meanwhile, heat the brandy or water with the peach preserve in a small pan, then brush the mixture over the top of the hot tart to glaze. Leave until quite cold, then wrap carefully and transport to the picnic in a rigid box.

63

Index